Business Intelligence in Plain Language

A practical guide to Data Mining and Business Analytics

By Jeremy M. Kolb

Applied Data Labs Inc.
Chicago, IL

Visit us on the web: www.AppliedDataLabs.com

Chicago, IL

Be sure to get your free copy of "What is Analytics?"

As a thank you for purchasing *Business Intelligence in Plain Language*, I want to give you a great companion report: "What is Analytics?" for free. Where this book drills down into Business Intelligence and its applications, the analytics report explores the wide range of applications for these same principles. Please go to:
http://www.applieddatalabs.com/content/enjoy-your-free-gift to get this report for free as a thank you for your purchase.

Secrets of the Big Data Revolution

We create about 2.5 quintillion bytes of data daily and approximately 90% of all our worlds data has been created in the past 2 years. Our world is transforming as this data deluge knocks us out of our old ways and into a data driven reality. Some companies are winning in this evolving world while others are falling behind. Big Data promises to give us a world driven by information with far greater productivity, increased profits, and lower costs and in *Secrets of the Big Data Revolution* we explore those winning strategies and the tools behind them.

Want to learn how companies like Amazon, Target, and IBM use data to gain competitive advantages? Or how Obama used Big Data tools to better utilize his resources? Get *Secrets of the Big Data Revolution* and learn about the driving forces behind this influential change.

TABLE OF CONTENTS

Introduction: Why Haven't Computers Enslaved us yet?   **10**
   How to use this Book   12

Chapter 1: So what is Business Intelligence?   **13**

Chapter 2: Dissecting the Mechanical Turk, What can Traditional Business Intelligence do?   **17**
   Outlier Detection   18
   Pattern Recognition   20

Chapter 3: Peering into the future, what is Business Intelligence learning to do now?   **23**
   Clustering   24
   Predictive Modeling   26
   Summarizing   27

Chapter 4: Implementing Business Intelligence - Getting the Data   **29**
   Data Transformation   32
   Data Cleansing and Normalization   32
   Data Integration Gotchas   33

Chapter 5: What Business Intelligence Tools are There?   **35**
   Traditional BI   36
   Data Discovery   37

Selecting a Tool   39

Chapter 6: Launching your BI solution   41

Appendix A: Sample chapter from *Secrets of the Big Data Revolution*   44

Appendix B: Business Intelligence further explored.
**   51**
Breaking it down   54
So what is Business Intelligence?   56

Appendix C: What is Big Data?   58

Appendix D: Data Mining   59
So how does Data Mining work?   60
What can Data Mining Do?   61

Appendix E: Term Glossary   62

Introduction: Why Haven't Computers enslaved us yet?

In May of 1997, the world awoke to a new reality: Chess Grandmaster Garry Kasparov lost to the supercomputer Deep Blue. To the public, this was the dawn of the computer era, where artificial intelligence would regularly trounce human intellect. To many it was the end of the line, the nail in the coffin for human intelligence. However, it is 15 years later and artificial intelligence isn't the driving force in politics or business. Why not?

As much as Deep Blue's victory is a set piece of computing history, a more recent match deserves it's time in the spotlight. In 2005 a chess tournament took place which allowed men to partner with machine. Those who thought Deep Blue was the final word were shocked as grandmasters with simple laptops defeated the supercomputers routinely and in the end, two amateurs with their three laptops won. Not the grandmasters with the supercomputers, but the amateurs who understood best how to utilize the tools they had.

Business intelligence is a tool just like the chess programs those amateurs ran. It isn't about computing power or about superior knowledge; it is about the relationship between you and your program. And it is the tool that can help you use data to beat back your biggest foes.

This book will teach you about business intelligence (BI) - how it works, the ideas behind it, and what you need to know to make the absolute most of your investment. We are going to be covering the five basic steps of BI: purpose identification, data cataloguing, data integration, Business Intelligence Tool selection, and finally deployment. Although these steps lend themselves to a sequential path in theory, in practice the process is more cyclical until you get the results you want. Through this book you will learn about each one of these steps in turn, and by the end of it you'll know enough to give those grandmasters a run for their money.

How to use this Book

I designed this book to be your tool. Your tool for understanding Business Intelligence: What it is, how it is used, and how you can get the most out of it. With that in mind the book is loaded with information, some of which provides a simple introduction to the concepts of BI and other areas providing behind the scenes stuff only data scientists really understand. In an effort to make this a simple topic to cover, the complicated explanations of concepts such as Big Data and Inductive Analytics are in the appendices at the end of the book. So if at any time you're feeling like you just need to know more about some of these concepts, just look through the appendices.

Chapter 1: So what is Business Intelligence?

One day a man walked into Asgard Inc. and changed the company forever. Unlike anyone who came before, he remembered and understood data as naturally as a fish swims in water. The CEO was shocked at how well the man knew the company. He started posing questions to this man. Who are my best customers? Why is this product struggling? Where is my greatest growth happening? The man answered these and more. Using his understanding of data, he identified key new markets, he discovered the best places to invest capital, and he even predicted the future. Overnight Asgard Inc. changed. Where before the CEO relied on limited information and gut feelings, now true knowledge guided his actions. The CEO took the man's hand in gratitude and asked, "Who are you?" and he replied, "I am Business Intelligence."

Before diving headfirst into how to implement, use, and benefit from Business Intelligence (BI), let's take a moment to lay the groundwork of what it is and why it matters.

BI is also sometimes referred to as business analytics, decision support, or knowledge management, it encompasses the methods and tools businesses use to analyze and understand important data--both from internal sources like customer records and external sources like government and academic data. These are the tools that enabled Target to identify pregnant women with focused marketing and drug companies to identify previously unnoticed side effects of their drugs. BI makes use of data analysis ideas and tools to spot patterns, trends, and correlations within data that in turn help decision-makers make informed choices.

Business intelligence is usually differentiated from analytics by its focus. BI typically focuses on the intelligence needed to drive a business, while analytics is slightly more abstract and focuses on the manipulation of the data itself--the algorithms, processes, and techniques used to derive the information. In fact you could probably look at business intelligence as the end product of analytics, when analytics is applied to business data.

BI has proven itself many times over to be a true asset in the business world. It helps companies increase profits, lower expenses, react faster, and anticipate situations. It can automate labor intensive data management, facilitate collaboration, and identify key performance indicators. And it can do so much more, as we'll see.

But before doing anything with BI, we need to stop and think about our goal first. It is so easy to get caught up in the buzz over data right now. As you read this book, you need to keep one clear goal in mind: generating Data Intelligence.

Data Intelligence is something I talk about quite a bit because so many people are doing BI for BI sake, and in the end that might just end up costing a lot of money without giving you much back in return. Data intelligence is a broad term that describes the real, meaningful insights that can be extracted from your data — truths you can act on. The goal of any data exercise should always be to get the information out of the data that will help you run things better.

Data intelligence is real and remarkably important — and whether you realize it yet or not, it's the reason you're reading this book. The insights that can be gained are supremely valuable as evidenced by a myriad of stories about how real companies have used intelligence gleaned from their data to transform their businesses and their industries.

The types of data intelligence required to solve a specific problem will vary. There are several different types of data intelligence — we can even put them on a scale of "Data IQ":

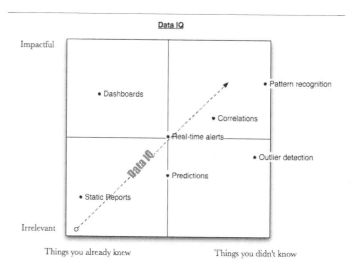

You get different types of information from each of these types of data intelligence. Of course your mileage may vary depending on your specific needs, and these tools can be combined or used alongside one another. For example pattern recognition and predictions could be incorporated into dashboards or real-time alerts.

Business Intelligence tools are phenomenal at making static reports, dashboards, and real-time alerts, and when you know the right questions to ask, these tools can truly help you make great use of your data.

All of these are examples of data intelligence. Right now the types of data intelligence in the upper-right quadrant of the chart are hard to get, and very complex. But as the field of business intelligence and data discovery tools mature, this will quickly change and using these types of data intelligence will be a competitive necessity.

Chapter 2: Dissecting the Mechanical Turk, What can Traditional Business Intelligence do?

There was once a young manager who was rummaging through a supply closet one day and found a dusty old oil lamp. He thought this was odd, so he grabbed a monitor-cleaning wipe and started cleaning the lamp. Out popped a genie who offered to grant him 3 wishes related to his current work. The manager told the genie he'd get back to him after he set up a conference call to discuss this with his boss and peers.

Sometimes knowing what you want is the hardest part. And it's no different with business intelligence. BI isn't a magic wand you wave over your data and it starts producing money, you have to know what you want and then seek it out to get the returns you are looking for. You need to ask yourself a few questions to start: What do I want to ask of my data? What are my objectives for this project? These are both good starting questions from which you can explore your data with purpose. You need to identify why you need BI.

Note: There is a class of BI tool called Data Discovery Tools that help you with this. These tools allow you to explore your data and find interesting aspects, ideas, and trends that you can then dive deeper into the information. We will have fun with this later, but if you want an in depth look at these tools check out our whitepaper on the topic at by clicking here.

As you read through this first section it's not a bad idea at all to take some notes. What you really want after you get done is a list of ideas; what information or knowledge you don't have but want your business intelligence solution to deliver. Jot down any ideas that pop into your head about things you'd like to know but don't today. Hopefully reading will prompt some internal brainstorming and you'll be way ahead of the game when it comes time to implement your BI solution.

In order to know what BI can do for you, you need to know a bit about what BI does from a slightly technical perspective. We'll take this in bite-sized chunks--let's first consider some of the earliest applications of BI: Outlier Detection and Association Rule Learning.

Outlier Detection

Have you ever gotten a call from your credit card company asking you to verify recent purchases? The reason they do that is because you establish a pattern of spending that rarely changes. When a purchase is made that is out of the ordinary, a notification is sent to the fraud prevention department asking them to follow up with you to see if the abnormal purchase was valid, or if the card was possibly stolen. This is outlier detection in action.

Outlier detection--sometimes called anomaly detection--is the process of identifying outliers in data or information that stands out from the rest. These outliers can represent errors in your data or they may be areas that you should focus on because they represent opportunity. Further investigation in these areas can lead to significant improvements when acted upon.

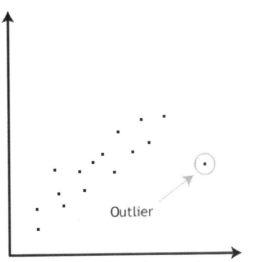

Some outliers can be easily spotted on a chart

There are several interesting common uses for outlier detection:

Opportunity identification -- When an outlier is remarkably better than the norm, you'll want to find out exactly *why* it was so much better. This is where you'll want to look at the differences between the outlier and the rest of your data to find the differences (something BI tools will typically help with).

Problem identification -- Conversely, outliers can also represent problems that need to be addressed.

Idea generation -- Outliers are particularly useful simply because they're *not* ordinary. Often just looking at how they're different will trigger ideas that you hadn't thought of before, which can then help you think of other questions you should be asking.

Fraud detection -- As described above, outliers are often selected for scrutiny and verification as a way of detecting and rooting out fraud.

Data Purity -- Data error can come from input problems or intentional malfeasance. In large data sets you can't manually identify these so outlier detection will find them so they can be fixed.

If you were running a retail store and did some outlier detection, you might find that 40% of your income comes from 5% of your customers who all live in the same area. Using this information you can then market to that area more heavily in order to drive those customers back and possibly grab some new high value customers. Or you might be able to locate new areas that are similar and present good opportunities that you should explore.

Of course, your mileage may vary depending on the industry you're in or unique quirks about your business. You may even find new uses for it that no one has even thought of yet-- that's the reason why it's important to understand what these techniques actually do.

Pattern Recognition

One of the core things BI tools should help you do is identify patterns. This is the process of discovering relationships within your data, finding correlations and possible causations. These relationships can show opportunities normally overlooked, cause-and-effect relationships you weren't aware of, and potential points of leverage that you should be thinking about.

Pattern recognition has many real-world uses that you might not be aware of. For example, grocery stores discovered many years ago that there's a segment of their customers who would purchase beer and diapers together--identifying that correlation allowed them to up potato chip sales by placing them between the diapers and beer. Pattern recognition is also used to identify human faces in photographs, computer-aided diagnostics in medicine, and spam prevention.

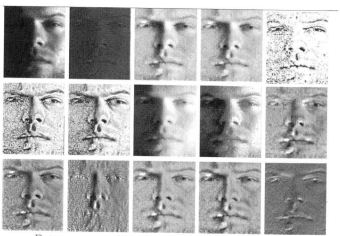

Pattern recognition is commonly used for facial
recognition

Pattern recognition is an umbrella term that covers a
whole array of algorithms--things like correlation,
regression, Bayesian predictions, and more. However,
many of today's BI tools address pattern recognition by
showing you data in graphical form using charts and
graphs and letting you pick out the patterns visually. Each
tool will approach this in a different way.

Using outlier detection and pattern recognition businesses
have identified opportunities and problems that would
have otherwise been ignored. And we are constantly
advancing the technology, exposing new opportunities
and finding better ways to get value from data.

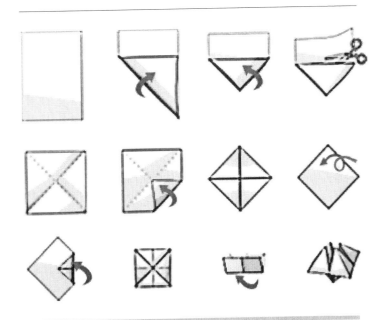

Chapter 3: Peering into the future, what is Business Intelligence learning to do now?

A king once visited a fortune teller who told him that his favorite dog would die that year. Sure enough, the dog died, and the king thought the fortune teller had caused it in some way. So he called her in front of him, enraged, and said "do you know when *you* will die?" She paused a moment and answered "yes, your majesty, exactly three days before you do!"

Predicting the future is one of the sexier applications of business intelligence, but unfortunately it doesn't quite work like a fortune teller. It's time we explore some remarkable and slightly misunderstood applications of business intelligence, predictions and clustering. In fact, these might properly be called part of *analytics*, which is similar to business intelligence but focuses more on the underlying algorithms.

Most raw data is not very useful to us. It is a mess of numbers with little explanation and gaining value from it is like searching for a piece of hay in a stack of needles, difficult and painful. Most of the data is not very useful to you, and finding the data that is useful can be a challenge. However, BI tools and techniques can make the task of understanding and using data to your advantage much simpler. Consider Clustering, Predictive Modeling, and Summarizing. These are the tools that are used to remove the needles from the haystack.

Clustering

In March of 2012, a paper was published in the renowned journal *Science* describing how scientists had been able to identify previously unknown drug interactions by using complaint data submitted to the FDA. Many of these interactions only manifested themselves in certain types of people, however, making it a tricky process. They were able to accomplish this feat using clustering.

Clustering is the process of discovering similar groups and structures within your data that enable you to more easily see relationships. Typically this is done in the background by an analytics tool that employs linear algebra techniques, but clusters can also been seen visually using charts like this:

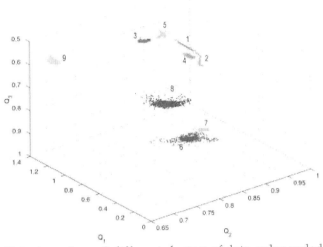

This chart shows 9 different clusters of data, color-coded

Market research relies heavily on cluster analysis when working with multivariate data such as surveys and test panels. Marketers use clusters to move the respondents into market segments, and then address the market segments rather than the individuals, thus enabling better understanding of how those segments respond. So if you were marketing Calvin and Hobbes legendary "Chocolate Covered Sugar Bombs" breakfast cereal, clustering would allow you to segment your market into parents, adults, young adults, teenagers, and kids in order to see what each segment thinks about the cereal. This would then allow you to tailor your marketing to each group.

However, you have to be careful when using clustering because some data just does not cluster well. Some data just doesn't lend itself well to the underlying math. This is especially true when you have very few data points to work with--say, less than 50 data points--or when you have so many variables that it there become an almost infinite number of clusters. Your analytics tool should help identify if the data is suitable for clustering or not.

Predictive Modelling

Everyone who hears about analytics and business intelligence typically wants to be able to do one thing: predict the future. This isn't a bad goal to have as long as you go in with the right expectations and prepare yourself for the possibility that the predictions may be wrong. Typically your predictions will arrive with a certain margin of error--they will be accurate with a 75% probability, for example. This is great when you're dealing with a large number of predictions (for a large customer base, for example), but not so great when you're dealing with a single prediction on its own.

Predictive modeling is the underlying process that tools use to make predictions. In practice, this works in one of two ways: it can look at current trends within your business and project into the future telling you what to expect in those important fields, or it can analyze your data with a particular future in mind and give the probability of that future coming true. When this tool is used alongside others it can enable you to see how certain changes will affect the probability of your goal outcomes.

One area where this directly affects you is within the insurance industry where predictive modeling has long been the standard used to determine premiums. Given the data they have collected from years of back customer records, they can predict your risk level with significant reliability and adjust your premiums accordingly.

Predictive modeling is usually considered an advanced technique, and is just now starting to mature to full potential. Not all BI software can do predictive modeling and few can do it well.

Summarizing

Often you won't want to look at your data at the most granular level available. For example, you probably won't want to look at individual sales if you have hundreds or thousands a day. Rather, you'll want to look at a summary of the sales by day, week, month, or year. Only by looking at your data from a higher level can you really get the perspective that you're after.

Summarization combines smaller packets of data into larger ones and provides a simple concise view of your data through visualizations and interactive tools. In summarizing your data, BI tools take the information gathered from clustering, predictive modeling, and the rest in order to provide understanding of your data. Infographics are perhaps the best known and simplest example of good summaries of data, their goal is to educate you about the data being presented.

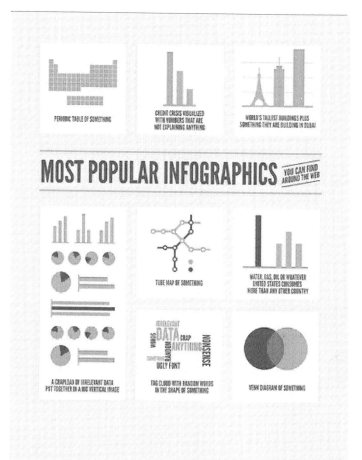

Understanding these tools should enable you to decide what you want to do with your data, and after deciding you can begin cataloging and evaluating.

Chapter 4: Implementing Business Intelligence - Getting the Data

Hopefully by now you have a good idea of what you want to be able to accomplish or answer with your business intelligence solution. If not, you may want to go back and re-read the last few sections, because as we mentioned before, knowing what you want is half the battle. We're now going to move into the *how*, how to design and implement your BI solution.

The first step in any BI endeavor is to know what you have to work with. Many organizations have data, but there's no definitive source of answers about what's there, where it is, and who owns it. Other organizations already have data warehouses that catalogue all the data in the company.

One of the hardest things to do after identifying the questions you want to ask is figuring out what data is needed to answer them. This requires some form of data catalog to work from, and if it doesn't exist it will need to be created.

You'll need to know:

1. What data is available (the objects and properties--or fields and tables--that are in the data)

2. What form the data is currently in (is it available in a database? As an export from a product? Via connecting to an API?)

3. How often can you get fresh data? An API will typically give fresh data, while an export might only get updated once a day.

If you realize your data is not sufficient to answer your questions, then what you have is an Information Gap. This gap is the difference between what data you have and what data you need. After identifying this gap, you then have to determine how much of the gap needs to be filled from internal sources and how much can be filled externally. This will heavily depend on what question you are answering. If you want to know about demographics for example, you can use external sources such as census data and other publicly available research. However, if you're looking to figure out which departments in your own company provide the best value, you are of course going to need to gather all the data internally. Many questions will fall somewhere between those two extremes and necessitate gathering data in both ways.

There are many sources of external data that you can explore to plug your information gaps. Here are a few to get you going:

Infochimps is perhaps the leading data marketplace, offering data on everything from Twitter to energy consumption.

Microsoft Azure Data Market offers many different types of data including real estate, transportation, consumer goods, and many more.

Pew Research, the famous survey-taking company that is often quoted on the news, offers many of its data sets for download and use.

There are many other data markets, but this should be enough to get you started.

Once all the data you need is gathered it needs to be integrated. This process is often called Data Warehousing and involves fixing any problems with the data, making data from different sources work together, and connecting the data to the BI tools being used.
Some BI tools (which we'll discuss later) offer lightweight data-warehousing capabilities built-in so that you don't have to go through this exercise. However, note that often these tools don't include the whole range of capabilities and are often limited as to the amount of data they can handle. So if you're planning on analyzing a *lot* of data you'll probably need to build an actual data warehouse.

Data warehouse projects are not cheap--they can often run into the hundreds of thousands of dollars--so be sure you need to undertake this to answer your questions before beginning. You may want to talk to a data consultant (or you could always email info@applieddatalabs.com, we'd be happy to chat) to help understand the scope of what you're looking at.

Data Transformation

The first step in using the data you've collected is turning it into a usable form, and putting it somewhere where a BI tool can get to it for analysis. Typically this means turning the data into tabular form of some kind--tools can typically even consume Excel files, for example.

The data will need to be stored somewhere, and this is typically a database. There are many different kinds of databases such as Microsoft SQL, Oracle, MySQL, and many, many more. The cost and capabilities of these vary wildly, but BI tools can talk to most of them. You'll want to select one that fits your needs and data size requirements.

Data Cleansing and Normalization

Most data sets have problems--they include a lot of data coming from people typing things into computers and recording things. There are misspellings, duplicates, missing data, and all kinds of other issues. The first step when treating data for use in business intelligence is data cleansing--fixing these problems as much as possible.

Typically this is not done by hand, but by an Extract, Transform, and Load (ETL) tool. These tools are the foundation of a data warehouse in that they are responsible for putting the data into the warehouse (after cleansing and normalizing it).

Data normalization is the process by which multiple sources of data are made to be similar. Take, for example, a data source which has sales data by day, and another data source which has sales data by week. You can't just join them because the data won't match; you'll first have to change the daily data into weekly data so you're dealing with the same type of data. This is called normalization, and is typically handled with ETL tools.

Data problems will affect the quality of the answers BI can give you, and therefore you want to make sure the data is as clean as possible. After all, when making important business decisions you don't want to be relying on "garbage" information.

Phew! Still with me? I know this a good bit of dry technical stuff but it is incredibly important. The old adage 'garbage in, garbage out' applies to data analysis like the Ten Commandments to the Israelites. Don't worry; we're getting to the fun stuff I promise. Soon you'll be dominating your data problems and using some awesome tools to find those opportunities you've been missing out on. Just hang in there.

Data Integration Gotchas

There are a few things you should be aware of going into a data warehousing or integration project. These are common things that trip up these efforts so you'll want to keep them in mind as you work with the people who control the data.

Connectivity. Often different data sources will require some connectivity between them, especially if they live in different parts of the organization. For example, integrating sales data with customer service data requires access to the data of both organizations, and connecting them to your data warehouse. This will require the cooperation of the data owners.

Security. You'll want to be aware of security through the entire process, as much data is sensitive and shouldn't be exposed to everyone. You'll need to track how sensitive each bit of data is and give special precautions to keep that data secure, especially if you need to pull it into the analysis tool.

Overlap. Often multiple systems within an organization will store the same data, sometimes in slightly different ways. You'll need to discuss this overlap with both parties and figure out which version is more trustworthy, or the rules about when to use which version.

Service disruptions. Keep in mind that systems do go down, and connectivity is lost sometimes. You'll want to develop a plan and make sure that if you're developing a data warehouse that it can recover gracefully.

Of course, this all depends on how sensitive or urgent your data analysis is. If it's not a big deal if something fails and you don't get your information for a day or two, then you probably don't need to be as cautious.

Chapter 5: What Business Intelligence Tools are there?

The current BI industry is roughly divided between two types of tools: traditional BI reporting tools and data discovery tools. The players in this market will typically have some traditional BI functions and some data discovery, and they change their functionality regularly. Here, I am going to cover both types of tools without looking at specific examples, but for a complete rundown of the current tools available I suggest reading our resources page:

http://www.applieddatalabs.com/content/business-intelligence-analytics-solutions-overview

Traditional BI

Traditional BI focuses on monitoring what is currently happening in your business and reporting on the findings. It focuses on enabling effective reporting and building dashboards that properly monitor your Key Performance Indicators (KPI). Let's start with traditional BI.

KPI

Key performance indicators are metrics--they are computed numbers that typically combine one or more underlying raw data numbers. For example, you might have a KPI that is the cost per customer, which would involve dividing the total marketing costs by the number of customers obtained.

BI tools focus on a particular area of a business such as customer retention, production cost analysis, or employee productivity (among others), and provides a detailed analyses of all the factors affecting that area. The goal is to provide a clear picture of what is happening and thereby give the user the knowledge necessary to then realize possible solutions and improvements. Reports are specifically tailored to request being made and are generated only when a request is put forth. In this way they are somewhat brittle because they require some development effort in order to answer a new question.

Dashboard

On the other hand, dashboards are often generated in real-time and monitored on a daily, weekly, or monthly basis. Often contained on a single page, a Dashboard provides an easy to understand graphical representation of a company's KPI's. Whereas reporting provides a detailed look at a small aspect of a business, Dashboards provide an overview of large segments.

Traditional BI has proven itself to be a useful tool capable of providing good returns on investment. Because of the complexity of generating reports and building dashboards in these systems, a dedicated IT department is typically needed to keep traditional BI tools humming. The new trend in BI is Data Discovery which we are going to explore next.

Data Discovery

Data discovery tools began emerging in the market in 2010 in response to the unmet ease-of-use and rapid deployment demands of business users. They aim to provide an interactive and graphically based user experience, and are becoming quite popular among those who aren't interested in the technical side of data analytics.

Data Discovery is much more diverse than traditional BI. Think of it as the rogue of the BI world: cool, interesting, sexy, and far more intuitive than the nerdy business type BI with its clean cut, tucked in approach that appeals to the older generation. Data Discovery allows you to do things traditional BI can't do, such as answer impromptu questions, and each Data Discovery tool has different abilities. In addition to many other features, you can generally count on Data Discovery to use a Data Visualization interface and enable Ad Hoc Queries.

It's important to note that for most companies Data Discovery isn't a replacement for Business Intelligence. There are certain needs within an organization that BI simply does very well. Instead, Data Discovery is often used to augment current BI solutions. It's like buying a high end tablet PC, it isn't going to replace your laptop, but it sure makes checking your email and googling on the fly easier.

"Ad Hoc"

Ad hoc basically means impromptu; something that was not scripted or developed in advance. The term has grown in use because traditional BI tools have very limited capacity in this area; they typically only allow you to filter the report you're looking at in different ways, not to create new reports based on your query. In BI the term has grown to incorporate speed and ease of use as well. Data Discovery tools enable users to make highly informed decisions about everything by using ad hoc queries.

Data Visualization

BI used to rely on individuals with high levels of technical and statistical abilities who were able to look at data and understand the implications of that information. With advancements in data visualization, those patterns are now accessible to a wider audience. What data visualization does is provide context, history, and future projections to your current data in a simplistic and interactive way. It allows you to explore your data, looking at what you think is important and allowing you to examine how small changes are likely to affect your whole business. It's sometimes referred to as "follow your nose analytics". It also makes data way more fun.

Where traditional BI provides a time tested and traditional approach to data management, Data Discovery is the new kid on the block with a new look and new approach. Data Discovery tools are quickly infiltrating the BI market.

Selecting a Tool

Earlier we talked about how to identify what type of questions you want your BI solution to answer, and how to make sure you have the data needed to answer them. Now you need to make sure that the tool you select is capable of answering those questions given the data. There is a laundry list of capabilities all BI providers will have, but there are a few key areas you'll want to ask about while looking for the right BI solution.

Can the tool identify outliers? Most tools will be able to plot a chart of your data, but that leaves you having to identify outliers on your own--after picking the right chart to look at. Some tools will identify outliers for you.

How much data can it handle? If you have a lot of data (on the order of gigabytes) some tools will simply fall apart under the load. Make sure that the tool is capable of handling as much data as you need.

Can the tool make predictions? If you want to make predictions you're going to need some support from the tool. Identify the predictions you want make using your data and make sure your tool is capable.

Will you need training? Many of the most capable tools are targeted at data scientists, not end users. Unless you're ok with that, understand what kind of training is required to use the tool.

Does it include data warehousing capabilities? If not, be aware and decide if you need a separate warehouse or not to integrate your data.

Do changes require development time? Many tools require developers to make changes, but data discovery tools are less likely to require this. Be aware.

You'll need to explore the features and use cases of the tools you're looking at to determine which category it falls into, or refer to the tools page on our site for a helping hand.

Chapter 6: Launching your BI solution

Most of the hard work is done, and you're almost ready to reap the rewards of your efforts. You know the questions you want to answer, you have the data you need, in the place you need it, and you have the tool that can answer those questions. But before you can learn all the ins and outs of your business you need to cover a few logistical necessities.

Security. If the data you're analyzing is sensitive, you'll want to make sure that the data warehouse doesn't let any unauthorized people see data they shouldn't. This is typically done at the data warehouse level, but is also a part of some BI tools.

Training. Many BI tools require a bit of training to use. You'll want to make sure that all of the end users in your organization receive the training.

Sales. Sales? Yes, sales. You'll want to show off your BI solution. Send out some reports to your colleagues, and show them what you can do now. It's the single best way to get other people using the solution you worked so hard on!

Congratulations! You now know the steps from conception to deployment that make any BI installation a success. Now you can turn your business data from a storage liability into a dynamic asset. Way to be awesome my friend. This isn't the end all of BI, but it is a starting point enabling you to know more about the procedures and utilization of BI in a way few outside the business understand.

Now throughout the process of choosing and implementing a BI system, you are going to need to review this information so that you know the questions to ask and the procedures needed to be completed--keep in mind, the more you understand the better your results will be.

We also want to help you continue to learn about BI, so we offer a weekly newsletter focusing on the state of the industry, key concerns all BI implementers face, and the amazing potential good BI solutions offer to business owners. If you would like to continue your BI education, sign up on our website: www.AppliedDataLabs.com.

I would love to hear your feedback and your questions, so feel free to email me at: Jeremy@AppliedDataLabs.com

Appendix A: Sample chapter from *Secrets of the Big Data Revolution*

Section 1.4: Learning Customer Secrets

At a Target outside of Minneapolis an angry father burst in demanding to talk with the manager. He was clutching a mailer sent to his teenage daughter. He didn't understand how Target could be so immoral as to send teenage girls ads for baby clothes and cribs. "Are you encouraging her to get pregnant?!" he indignantly asked. The manager looked at the mailer and quickly understood the father's anger. Cute babies and pregnant mothers on the cover of an ad with coupons for maternity clothes and baby formula. The manager apologized profusely and assured the father he would look into it personally and it would not happen again.

One of the offers the daughter received

A few days later the manager called the father to apologize again for the company's error, but instead it was the fathers turn to say he was sorry. "It turns out there's been some activities in my house I haven't been completely aware of. She's due in August. I owe you an apology."

Statisticians get asked some weird questions, and for Target's Andrew Pole, his came from marketing: "If we wanted to figure out if a customer is pregnant, even if she didn't want us to know, can you do that?"

What? Why would they want to know that?

And this is where it gets really interesting, and where conventional psychology plays into the data mining process. People build habitual lives, they go to the same places, shop at the same stores, and build comfortable routines for themselves. It's hard to change these life patterns; to get people to start shopping at your store and stop going to that other one. But psychologists have discovered that there are certain times in a person's life when these patterns are more susceptible to alteration, big life changes like becoming pregnant trigger these susceptible times.

Ever since marketers learned of this, they've been trying to target customers before, during, and after these experiences, and companies like Target are fighting over these customers to try to gain any advantage they can. That's why Pole came up with the "Pregnancy Prediction" so Target might know a few weeks before their competition that a mother is expecting.

If Target could find these customers during this period of flux, they had an opportunity to capture them for the rest of their lives.

"We knew that if we could identify mothers in their second trimester, there's a good chance we could capture them for years," said Pole. "As soon as we get them buying diapers from us, they're going to start buying everything else too. If you're rushing through the store, looking for bottles, and you pass orange juice, you'll grab a carton. Oh, and there's that new DVD I want. Soon, you'll be buying cereal and paper towels from us, and keep coming back."

So Pole and his team got to work, mining through vast data warehouses and public records. They explored past records of customers known to have had a child and looked for purchasing trends among them that could predict pregnancy. Soon the patterns emerged. Unscented lotions and soaps, cotton balls, zinc and magnesium supplements, and vitamins, these are among the 25 products Pole used to build a predictable pattern expecting mothers would follow. These products formed the basis for Targets "Pregnancy Prediction", a prediction providing a pregnancy percentage likelihood that even estimates a mother's due date. Soon after this was built, Target started sending ads based on expected due date.

This Data Science project was wildly successful for Target. Minus a few hiccups like the teenager in Minneapolis. It turns out pregnant women, much like all of us, don't like the feeling of being spied on so Target made some changes to its program to avoid the creepiness factor. They found out that if they added innocuous items such as laundry soap next to the pregnancy sales people didn't feel as targeted. They just added a touch of randomness to the mailers. With wineglass coupons next to vitamin supplements and garage door openers next to baby diapers, Target stopped creeping out customers and started winning loyalty.

How it Works

Target is a company that knows the value of continually enriching data, and that's how they're able to pull off tricks like identifying pregnant women by their buying patterns. Target maintains a database of customers, and if you've ever shopped at Target you're in it. It keeps a list of each credit card and email address a customer uses, and a complete list of purchases they've ever made. Since they maintain this customer record and complete history, and they can also track when women sign up for a gift registry for a baby shower, they have a fairly accurate indication of changing buying patterns leading up to a woman registering for baby gifts.

Pole was able to identify about 25 products that, when analyzed together, allowed him to assign each shopper a "pregnancy prediction" score. More important, he could also estimate her due date to within a small window, so Target could send coupons timed to very specific stages of her pregnancy.

For example imagine a woman that suddenly buys cocoa-butter lotion, a purse large enough to double as a diaper bag, zinc and magnesium supplements and a bright blue rug. That information can be used to assign a prediction score of say, 75 to the chance that she's pregnant, and you can guess fairly accurately when she's due within a month or two of those purchases.

How to Do it

There are a few ways to obtain this sort of insight from data. One is trial and error, having a data scientist do a manual classification exercise where he looks at known cases of pregnant customers and attempts to divine patterns from them, testing hypotheses against known good data. However, this approach is very manual, doesn't scale well, and notably requires a data scientist.

Another approach uses what is called a Sequence Clustering Algorithm, which is an algorithm that attempts to find common paths, or sequences, which lead to specific events. Typically these algorithms are run against time-based event data, such as buying habits. Other data sets that are great candidates for sequence clustering algorithms include:

o   -Click paths that are created when users navigate or browse a Website.
o   -Logs that list events preceding an incident, such as hard disk failure or server deadlocks.
o   -Records that follow customer (or patient) interactions over time, to predict service cancellations or other poor outcomes.

Sequence Clustering Algorithms vary in their implementations, but almost all of them use some variation of Markov Chain Analysis (which you can learn more about on our resource page or in appendix A). Markov chains are used to determine the probabilities of something moving from one state to another by using a set of training data and determining the distances (using distance calculations, which we will look at in section 1.6) between all possible sequences, and using those distances to determine the sequences that best represent real-world buying patterns for similar customers (or click paths, or log events, or interactions, etc.).

Jargon Watch
"Training data" is data with some known properties — specifically, you know that it contains examples of the outcome looking for. Not all algorithms require training data, but the ones that do learn how to act by trying to extract rules from the training data that you give them — these rules are then called a "model".

Markov chains are interesting algorithms useful for many different things in computer science. They essentially analyze and predict the probability that something will go from one state to another. For example, they are sometimes used to create computer-generated text by calculating the most probable word to follow another, or to follow the previous sequence of words. This results in often entertaining computer-generated gobbledygook such as the following:

Can you put a few years of your twin-brother Alfred, who was apt to rally round a bit. I should strongly advocate the blue with milk.

This text was generated by doing a Markov chain analysis of *My Man Jeeves* by Wodehouse: you can see that while it is complete nonsense it is also somewhat coherent nonsense, and if you're familiar with *My Man Jeeves*, you can see how this sentence might come from rules generated by analyzing that book. It doesn't understand the meaning of each step in the chain, but it does a decent job of stringing together links that might conceivably come after one another.

Get your copy of *Secrets of the Big Data Revolution* from Amazon today!

Appendix B: Business Intelligence further explored.

Although the term "Business Intelligence" is thrown around like beer in a frat house, it seems like few people are able to really describe its key functionality in simple terms. But luckily you bought this book.

So let's say John owns a chain of restaurants specializing in exotic meats and rainforest produce. He is going to have a lot of data coming in: data about his customers and data about his internal processes. That data will be in a bunch of different spreadsheets: invoice records in one place, individual restaurant performance numbers in another, income and expense data somewhere else, and a load of other numbers strewn across different systems. Without Business Intelligence and Data Warehousing this would simply be a cluster cuss of data sitting in his computers and costing him money.

The first part of BI is building a Data Warehouse. This will transform all of John's data into a commonly understood format and then store it in a centralized location. This allows John's data on exotic meat to be understood in the same way as his individual restaurant performance data. Once the data is consolidated in this way then BI can get to work.

What BI will do for John is crunch the numbers fast. For example, John can use data collected on his famous Sloth Burger-- cost, food spoilage data, and the pricing model-- then use BI to crunch the numbers and obtain the margins on the Sloth Burger for each of his restaurants. Taking it from there, he can drill down deeper and find that one restaurant is underperforming with Sloth Burgers. Using BI he can gather all of the relevant data about his burgers and view it all in one place. Order times, customer complaints, tips earned, time from order to table, ingredient inventory records, and whatever else might be applicable. Comparing the expected too the actual, he discovers that the stock of Shiitake mushrooms, a key ingredient, is higher than it should be when Alex is in charge of the kitchen... he must be messing up the recipe! Without BI he wouldn't have discovered this unless he happened to visit that restaurant when Alex was cooking and tried the burger. Instead of that complicated mess, he is able to discover the problem while sipping a mango tango in Hawaii.

One more quick example: Say John has a subscription service delivering monthly specialty foods. With all the customer data, he can identify the particular zip codes that provide the bulk of his subscriptions. That's cool right? Now he can focus his marketing on those zip codes. But with BI, he can take that information and learn much more. Using publicly available census data, he'll discover the common threads connecting his most popular zip codes, and he will even be able to research what other zip codes have those same features! BI just identified John's most promising new market.

Breaking it down

There are three major concepts of Business Intelligence (BI): Data, Data Warehousing, and Data Analysis. These three concepts are the basics of BI.

How should I understand Data?

Before exploring anything about BI you need understand the nature of the main resource it uses: Data. Data is any collection of numbers, facts, text, essentially any raw input that can be processed by a computer. Data is also a resource. It is quite similar to traditional resources such as copper or wool in that someone produces it, and then someone uses the raw material and makes something new from it. However, it is unique from traditional commodities because it doesn't get used up in the process, making it particularly interesting and uniquely valuable. Data can be produced by anyone, and with advancements in analytical technology can be utilized by everyone with the capital to invest in data analysis.

So what is Data Warehousing?

Data warehousing is the process of taking data from multiple sources, cleaning it up and making it uniform, and then placing it into a common storage area (the "data mart"). From there, the data mart can be used by business intelligence and analytics tools to look at all of the data from the different data sources as a whole--instead of as segregated data sources. It allows an apples to apples comparison instead of apples to oranges. From a technical perspective, a simple expression of what a data warehouse is looks like this:

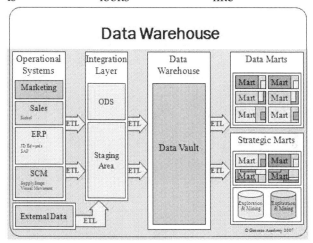

ETL: Extract, Transform, Load
ERP: Enterprise Resource Planning
SCM: Supply Chain Management
ODS: Operational Data Store

Just kidding--this is way more complicated than it needs to be. For the non-engineers among us, data warehousing is the process of integrating data from multiple sources into one uniform data source (Data Vault). This takes three simple steps referred to as Extract, Transform, Load--often referred to as ETL. First you take the data from one source (Extract), Change it into the data warehouses standard format (Transform), and then save it into the data warehouse (Load). That is all there is to it; that is data warehousing.

So what is Business Intelligence?

Definition: "Business Intelligence (BI) is the collection of technologies and processes that turns data into usable knowledge in order to inform decisions and drive action."

When I write about BI, I am typically talking about both of the two major types: Data Discovery and Traditional BI. Both types have their advantages, but Data Discovery is definitely the more exciting of the two. Where Traditional BI provides the tools to discover the answer if provided the proper question, Data Discovery finds the answer to the question you didn't think to ask. It is the advancement from deductive data analysis to inductive data analysis.

Deductive Data Analysis (Traditional BI)

Deductive data analysis is one of two means of analyzing data; it enables users to answer questions such as: What happened? When? Who? And How Many? Using tools such as Excel and OLAP, a user first makes an educated guess regarding the cause of a particular abnormality or trend. Then using deductive analysis tools the user is able to confirm or negate the validity of that hypothesis, and can form a new hypothesis to test if needed.

Inductive Data Analysis (Data Discovery)

Contrasting deductive data is inductive analysis. Instead of starting with a hypothesis, users are able to start with a goal and discover the data that informs that goal. Do you want to know what zip code is most likely to respond to your offer? Inductive analysis will find the data most applicable and give you the answer. Inductive analysis starts with the data and discovers the best parts of it to answer whatever question you put to it.

Appendix C: What is Big Data?

What is Big Data? It is a buzzword plain and simple. There is no uniformly accepted definition because people use the term to mean a wide variety of things to suit their purposes. It has been used to describe data tools, data sets, questions, problems and answers.

The way it is used most frequently by those in the industry- at least those who aren't pushing a particular agenda- also happens to be the most useful and simple understanding available: Big Data is data that is significantly large. In other words Big Data is big data, but let's break that down a bit starting with how we should understand data.

We covered this before but it is worth a refresher. Data is any collection of numbers, facts, text, essentially any raw input that can be processed by a computer. Data is also a resource. It is quite similar to traditional resources such as copper or wool in that someone produces it, and then someone uses the raw material and makes something new from it. However, it is unique from traditional commodities in that it doesn't get used up in the process, making it particularly interesting and uniquely valuable. Data can be produced by anyone, and with advancements in analytical technology, can be utilized by everyone with the capital to invest in data analysis.

The "Big" part of Big Data is a bit harder to define. Some put numerical qualifications to it, and others define it in regards of our ability to handle the sheer quantity or speed. However, it seems most practical to define Big Data in light of the situation that gave birth to the term in the first place.

What is Big Data then? Big Data refers directly to the current data situation, where the amount of data is growing so fast that we simply can't handle the sheer quantity. In 2010 Eric Schmidt, then CEO of Google, said that we now create as much data every 2 days as we did from the dawn of man through 2003. We are now producing far more data than we did in 2010. Pretty cool.

Keep an eye on our resources page as we are preparing to build a book around understanding Big Data in the near future.

Appendix D: Data Mining

In a very general sense, data mining (or data discovery, knowledge discovery) is the identification of correlations and patterns within data. These correlations and patterns provide insight into a company's decisions and help to understand their market better. Data mining identifies these patterns by analyzing data from a variety of angles.

Companies have been using data mining for a long time, but recent advancements in technology have made these processes significantly easier and better. These advancements allow companies to analyze ever increasing amounts of data in order to reduce costs and/or increase profits.

So how does Data Mining work?

The simplest way to understand Data Mining is in terms of data, information, and understanding.

Data is any collection of numbers, facts, text; essentially any raw input that can be processed by a computer. This data can be separated into three categories: Transactional/operational (accounting, inventory, customer profiles, etc.), Non Operational (forecast data, macroeconomic data, etc.), and Meta Data (data about data). Currently we produce so much data that there is a significant data overload stressing current data mining tools. For example, a supermarket has data about each customer's purchasing habits, overall inventory, pricing, sales, etc., which must be used to gain the next step: *Information*.

Information is the patterns and correlations among the data and provides the context for understanding. Data becomes information when it starts answering the questions of who, what, where, when, and how. The supermarket in the prior example demonstrates a regular pattern of increased beer and diaper sales on Thursday, with a correlation between the customers who buy these items: fathers of young children. The data leads to information about sales patterns, then gives way to usable knowledge, or *understanding*.

Understanding comes when information enables the forecasting and utilization of data to produce positive outcomes. Instead of just knowing what and where, you can identify the why and take advantage of it. The supermarket sales team identified this increase in beer and diaper sales were connected to young fathers getting ready for the weekend. The sales team then placed chips and other snacks between the diapers and beer. This is a good example of understanding; the sales team used the data to find information and understanding in order to drive snack sales.

What can Data Mining Do?

In today's business world, data mining is used by most large companies, with the most significant users in the financial, marketing, and retail industries. Data mining is used to analyze internal data such as expenses, staff performance, price, inventory, and external data such as competitors, the economy, and demographics. When these data streams are combined they enable companies to understand the importance of all of the data in relation to how the company is currently functioning. A company can then identify the key performance indicators to raise profits and cut spending.

So what is Data Mining? It is the process used by today's largest companies to grow intelligently and understand their businesses like never before. Data mining creates a system of understanding and integrating sources of data, allowing an organization to use these sources for its best interest. Data mining is becoming an extremely important tool in twenty-first century business.

Keep an eye on our resources page as we are preparing to build a book around Data Mining/Data Discovery in the near future.

Appendix E: Term Glossary

I went really light on the technical jargon for this book, but if you're looking to continue your study of business intelligence, you'll probably want to be familiar with these terms.

Ad Hoc Query
A data query issued in response to an immediate need requiring instant feedback.

Affinity Analysis
See Recommender Algorithm

Aggregate data
Data combined from multiple sources.

Basket Analysis
See Recommender Algorithm

Big Data
Umbrella buzzword under which a wide range of advancements in data management reside.

Cloud Computing
One form of computing as a service, often providing analytics services without requiring onsite installation.

Conversion Identifier
A value within a dataset that allows it to be joined with another related dataset.

Correlation

A value ranging from 1 to -1 that indicates the level to which two variables or values move together.

CRM (Customer Relationship Management)
CRM software provides basic BI abilities to small businesses

Dashboards
An old means of keeping track of data that presented groups of important data selected by the user.

Data
Anything that can be translated into a language a computer can understand.

Data Analysis
Using statistics, with or without the aid of computerized tools, to analyze data.

Data Analytics
Using statistics and data science tools to analyze data.

Data Cleaning
The removal of mistakes from a dataset.

Data Clusters
Groupings of data around particular characteristics.

Data Consumerization
The process of making data easy to use.

Data Cruncher
Any tool that helps people do data analytics.

Data Discovery
The analytics driven ability to play with data and find unique and valuable information.

Data Drilling
Breaking data into its component parts in order to gain greater insight. (days to hours, hours to minutes, etc.)

Data Intelligence
Clear usable information gathered through data analysis.

Data Mining
Designing of new processes for creating useful data intelligence.

Data Normalization
The act of changing the structure of different data sets so that they match. (Illinois –to- IL)

Data Pipeline
The process data goes through in order to be analyzed.

Data Query
The information (a question) sent to analytics software in order to gather data knowledge (an answer).

Data Reporting
The task of turning a data query into data knowledge that is now performed by analytics.

Data Semi – Structured
Data that has a structure under unstructured information.

Data Set

A collection of facts and figures, commonly in spreadsheet form, submitted to a program for analysis.

Data Story
The idea that, when understood properly, data tells useful stories.

Data Structured
Data that is fully suitable to be used by Analytics tools.

Data Unstructured
Information like video or text that requires translation prior to analysis.

Data Visualization
An emerging trend in analytics that enables easier proportional and relational analysis through the use of charts, graphs, and infographics.

Data Warehousing
The storing and managing of large amounts of data.

Data Wrangling
The skill of making various datasets work together well.

Database
A data storage center.

Decision Automation
New technology that enables analytics systems to make changes to optimize performance.

ERP (Enterprise Resource Planning)

Companywide uniform data management system providing real time data tracing and often automated decision making tools.

ETL (Extract Transform Load)
The process of taking data from an outside source, converting it to fit current standardization, and adding it to current data.

HOLAP (Hybrid Online Analytical Processing)
Combination of ROLAP (relational) and MOLAP (multidimensional) enabling higher degrees of control and data manipulation for the user.

Infographic
A data presentation style that aims to make data appealing to look at and visually punchy.

Insights
The truths hidden in data that can be used to improve the way a business in run.

Interactive Reporting
Data reporting tools with high levels of data discovery easily accessible.

KPI (Key Performance Indicators)
User selected data streams that indicate overall success. Typically a key component of dashboards.

KSI (Key Success Indicators)
See KPI

Machine learning algorithms

Algorithms that can learn from a given set of data, what to look for in other data.

MOLAP (Multidimensional Online Analytical Processing)
The more traditional form means of data storage for OLAP, faster processing but less data storage ability.

Metadata
The concept of data about data, most easily understood as reference tools.

Multidimensional Analysis
Data visualization demonstrating multiple factors of importance (volume and time, profit margin, expenses, revenue, time, etc.)

Multivariate Testing
Hypothesis testing on complex multi-variable systems.

Natural Language Processing (NLP)
The tools used to add structure to written or spoken language.

OLAP Online Analytical Processing
A technical term referring to specific background structures of analytics within cloud computing.

Outlier Detection
The identification of statistically valid deviations from the established norm for a given entity.

Pattern recognition
The process of Identifying and analyzing patterns within data.

Predictions
The process of making estimations of probable outcomes based on current data.

Real Time Alerts
Scorecard tool that enables you to receive instant notification if preset data values happen.

Recommender Algorithm
An Algorithm that analyzes patterns in data to find correlations that provide recommendations. Example: Amazon's "also bought" or "also viewed".

RDBMS (Relational Database Management System)
The technology enabling more rational organization of data.

ROLAP (Relational Online Analytical Processing)
A means of data storage that enables far greater amounts of data storage.

Root Cause Analysis
The process by which analytics identifies the initial cause of a statistical anomaly.

Scorecard
A data report tracking KPI's and comparing current level with set goals. Does not provide information on how to attain the goals however.

Sequence Clustering Algorithm
An algorithm that attempts to find common paths, or sequences, which lead to specific events.

Static Reports
Reports about data that are ordered, then processed and delivered.

Statistically Valid
A measure used to determine if a particular result is worth acting upon.

Statistics
The principles of data manipulation that are the driving force in data science.

Theoretical Analytics
The branch of analytical science focused on the expansion of analytical computing abilities.

Training Data
A set of data that has been classified as good, and is then used to train an algorithm to classify similar types of data.

Made in the USA
Lexington, KY
27 April 2014